To THE
MANCHESTER
LIBRARY

A COLD WIND FROM IDAHO

Best Wishes

LARRY
Matsuda

A Cold Wind From Idaho

poems

Lawrence Matsuda

with an introduction
and afterword by
Tetsuden Kashima

Black Lawrence Press
New York

Contents

Part III. No Longer Heroes

Black Lawrence Press
www.blacklawrence.com

Executive Editor: Diane Goettel
Book Design: Steven Seighman

Cover illustration detail from 'American Diary: August 17, 1942,' courtesy of Roger Shimomura.

Author photo by Tara Gimmer

Black Lawrence Press
115 Center Ave
Aspinwall, PA 15215
U.S.A.

Published 2010 by Black Lawrence Press, an imprint of Dzanc Books

ISBN: 978-0-9826364-0-4

First edition 2010

Printed in the United States

This book is dedicated to the following:

To my late mother and father, Hanae and Ernest K. Matsuda, who lived dignified lives, often under undignified circumstances. They lost their grocery business, their home, a stillborn child, and were incarcerated in Minidoka, one of ten American concentration camps during World War II. Their imprisonment lifted them, along with 120,000 other Japanese and Japanese Americans from their communities across America, without their having committed a crime and without due process.

To my Hiroshima relatives who told me their stories of survival when I visited them in 1995, which was the 50th anniversary of the atomic bombing: Mitsugi Yamada, Akiko Nagata, Yoko Tamino, Mitsuko Doi, and Isao Nishimura. Three Hiroshima poems deal with their stories. My mother lost many Hiroshima cousins, but my relatives who survived would not speak about them.

The deaths and suffering of over 500,000 civilians underscore the message of Hiroshima and Minidoka—let it not happen again. For my son Matthew's sake, school children all over America, and those who will choose never to let this happen in America again—it is my hope that this book becomes a reminder to America to fulfill its promise of liberty and justice for all, regardless of race, during times of war and hysteria. Numbers alone cannot adequately quantify the humiliation and shame that these poems address. Mindful of the anguish of those untold thousands who live on after such soul-tearing events, the families and friends who do not forget, and who re-suffer these losses and are unable to express or redress their losses—I write this book for them.

Thanks to my family—Karen Matsuda, Matthew Matsuda, Alan Matsuda, Tom Yamada, and Pamela Yamada Krute for their continued support. Thanks to Tess Gallagher for mentoring me on this journey, Carol Benge and Judith Skillman for their editing assistance. I am indebted to Linda Ando, Alfredo Arreguin, the late Professor Nelson Bentley, Carole Koura Kubota, Frank Kitamoto, Susan Lane, Susan Lytle, Professor Tets Kashima, and Roger Shimomura for their encouragement.

INTRODUCTION

President Franklin D. Roosevelt signed Executive Order 9066 on February 19, 1942, resulting in a cataclysmic series of events affecting all persons of Japanese ancestry then residing on the West Coast of the United States. So calamitous were these actions that a noted scholar asserted that this action constitutes "the defining event in the history of Japanese Americans."[1]

What does this have to do with a book of poetry titled, *A Cold Wind from Idaho*? Those Americans familiar with the Pacific Northwest Japanese American World War II experience will understand the imagery wrought by the title as being both evocative and apt. The metaphor of freezing winter winds chilling the body and then entering the soul of those affected conveys fittingly how the Japanese Issei[2] and Japanese American Nisei encountered, braved, and then survived the cold iciness of Idaho's winters while they were huddled in a primitive American barbed wire concentration camp.

---

1. Yamaoka, Kazue, "Japanese Americans," in Y. Jackson (editor), *Encyclopedia of Multi-cultural Psychology*. Thousand Oaks, CA: Sage Publications, 2006, p. 280.

2. Issei, or literally, "first-generation,' are the original Japanese nationals who emigrated to Hawaii and the continental United States from the late 1800s to 1924. Their children, the Nisei, literally, "second-generation," are American-born citizens; their grandchildren, the Sansei, literally, "third-generation," likewise are American-born citizens but were so young that few experienced the forced expulsion and incarceration in 1942.

It should be made clear from the beginning that the poetry in this volume is in many respects unlike the traditional Western oriented poems. The themes and the actors' actions in each poem are infused with the values and norms found in the Japanese American ethnic subculture. Moreover, without a clear understanding of the particular and peculiar set of historical and social relationships that the Issei and Nisei, as a group, faced with the majority society before, during, and after World War II, much of the actions and reactions of members of this ethnic group to the conditions of World War II may be less then easily comprehensible. For those who wish to understand the innermost values and norms of the Japanese Americans as they are exhibited with each piece will be rewarded by a careful reading of the following expressively written poetic presentations.

The purpose of this introduction is to provide historic information. The Afterwords section, however, provides a richer exploration of the cultural context as well as comments that hopefully, provide an appreciation and understanding of Japanese American values and norms embedded in the poems.

Issei and Nisei Internment and Incarceration

Many Americans know that during World War II, the United States government forcibly removed and incarcerated nearly 120,000 persons of Japanese American ancestry, two-thirds of whom were American citizens, without charge, trial, or other safeguards of an American legal system. This action encompassed all those then residing in the western half of Washington, Oregon, the southern half of Arizona and the entire state of California. In a nation where the legal foundation of "innocence until proven guilty" is paramount, all persons of Japanese ancestry, both American citizens and permanent resident nationals of Japan alike, were summarily expelled from their homes and suffered to remain in barbed wire enclosures for an unspecified period of time. They had committed no crimes or deeds inimical to the war efforts of their natal or adopted country; yet, unlike other Americans of German or Italian ancestry, they were forced to endure the horrendous fate of mass exclusion and imprisonment.

A salient originating moment for the World War II imprisonment starts with the bombing of Pearl Harbor.[3] Here, teams of Federal Bureau of Investigation agents, U.S. Army military police, and various local law enforcement officers fanned out throughout the United States and its Territories, such as Hawaii and Alaska, to execute the arrests of pre-designated resident aliens of Germany, Italy, and Japan under the authority of the Alien Enemies Act of 1798. After receiving a personal hearing, the Department of Justice and the U.S. Army placed individual aliens into Internment Centers and held most for at least the major portion of the war years.

In a separate but related set of actions, starting in May, 1942, under the authority of President Franklin D. Roosevelt's Executive Order 9066, the Army's Western Defense Command, responsible for the Western United States, selected fifteen temporary confinement sites in county fairgrounds, migrant labor camps, and horse race tracks—the latter sites still reeking with the aroma of horse manure—as temporary detention places it called "Assembly Centers." Here, they brought the remaining Issei nationals not apprehended in the example. In order to maintain order, camp authorities even erected an additional fenced-in enclosure within the larger barbed wire perimeter and urged for legislative action allowing American citizens to renounce their citizenship on American soil in time of war in order that such persons could then be interned into Justice Department centers and later deported as an "enemy alien."

The first WRA camp to close was the Jerome (Arkansas) Relocation Center in June, 1944 and the last was the Tule Lake

---

3. See Kashima, Tetsuden. *Judgment Without Trial: Japanese American Imprisonment during World War II*, Seattle: University of Washington Press, 2003.

(California) Segregation Center on March 20, 1946.[4] Within nearly four years of its existence– from the "Assembly Centers" of April 1942 until its closing – they contain the materials for an epic drama filled with strife and reconciliation, love and hate, benevolence and malevolence, anxiety and reassurance, and fear and security.

These issues comprise the larger tapestry of history and circumstances that encompass the Issei and Nisei experiences of World War II. Yet, each image is composed of individual threads that together weave into an artistic whole. The poems in this volume constitute threads of individual experiences without which there would be little comprehension or depth of understanding of the Japanese American's perspective. Equally important, those threads extend out to successive Japanese American generations who were fortunate not to have faced this particular anguish of their grandparents or parents. Yet, through no fault of their own, the Sansei and Yonsei generation may bear the poignant imagery crafted by Larry Matsuda that, "I carry my own fence. Barbed wire encircles me always."

Tetsuden [Tetsu] Kashima
University of Washington
Seattle, WA, 2010.
[Incarcerated, WRA "Relocation Center," 1942-1945]

---

4. Burton, Jeffrey F., Mary M. Farrell, Florence B. Lord, Richard W. Lord, *Confinement and Ethnicity: An Overview of World War II Japanese American Relocation Sites*, Seattle: University of Washington Press, 2002 (1999).

I.

The Noble Thing

They say when you die, your name
is written in the clouds.

—Anne from *Out of the Past*, 1947 RKO Pictures

Too Young to Remember

Minidoka, Idaho—War Relocation Center

I do not remember the Idaho winter winds,
knee deep mud that oppressed 10,000 souls
or the harsh summer heat and dust.

I do not remember miles of clotheslines,
mounds of soiled diapers, clatter of families crowded
into barracks, the greasy closeness
of canned Vienna sausage,
of pungent pork and sour brine
exuding from mess halls.

Floating in the amniotic fluid,
tethered in salt sea, odors
nourished by fear and sadness—
my Mother's anxieties
enveloped and nurtured me.

Maybe it was the loss of her home,
the sudden evacuation,
being betrayed by her country.
Or maybe it was the stillborn child
she referred to as It,
sexless blob of malformed tissue,
a thing without a face that would have been
my older sibling.
My aunt described it as *budo*,
a cluster of grapes.

I recall what Barry, my psychiatrist friend,
said about parents emotionally distancing themselves
from children born immediately after a stillbirth.

Sixty years later on drizzly Seattle days,
when November skies are overcast,
and darkness begins at 4:00 p.m.,
I feel my mother's sadness
sweep over me like a cold wind from Idaho.

I search for Minidoka,
unravel it from the memories of others.
Like a ruined sweater, I untwist the yarn,
strands to weave a tapestry
of pride and determination—
the "children of the rising sun" once banished
to desert prisons, return from exile
with tattered remnants, wave them overhead,
time-shorn banners salvaged from memories
woven in blood and anguish.

I wish I could remember
Minidoka. I would trade
those memories for the fear and sadness
imbedded in my genes.

The Noble Thing

Dad never talked about Minidoka.
That was the noble thing.

Before World War II,
there was Garfield High School for him,
ice skating on Greenlake,
dances at Lake Wilderness Lodge,
later his ownership of Elk Grocery
on Seneca Street.

He and my mother were
married in 1941,
ten months later to be removed
...forced...into the Minidoka concentration camp.

Mom was five months pregnant in August
with my older brother, Alan.
With black-out curtains drawn, the train
left Puyallup and climbed the Cascade mountains
until the land flattened and the inescapable sun
transformed the train cars into a moving sauna.
People gasped small, panicked breaths
from the superheated air.

Shikataganai—"It can't be helped."

The train stopped by the side of an unmarked road
in the Idaho desert, released
its passengers miles from any station.
Rumors spread they would be shot
or marched to death—their bodies stacked, then
carted to some awaiting ditch.

Nowhere to run, they walk in their best shoes
in the gritty sand as on the face of the moon.
The heat caused some to faint
as they carried all they could.

Three years later, Dad returned
to Seattle after the War,
developed a bleeding ulcer,
lost his janitor job at the Earl Hotel.

Depression took Mom away
like invisible armed guards. She was
a stranger—a stick-like figure with arms
and legs poking out of a white smock,
pacing the sidewalk next
to the Western State Hospital turn-around.

Dad never talked about it, none of it.
I never heard him say the word Minidoka...

Gaman, "endure the unbearable with dignity."

Shikatagani, my best friend's mother chose pills for suicide.
After school, Randy my neighbor, opened the garage door
and found his father in a black suit, his best, hanged
by the neck, *shikatagani*, the same path other
Seattle Japanese chose—
numbers unknown. *Shikataganai.*

We, however, never talked about it.
That was the noble thing to do.

Therapy

I wish you learned to cry for yourself.
You don't pay me enough to cry for you.
            —Leslie, my therapist

            i

If this scene were a Freudian dream,
her basement furnace pipes
extending throughout the house
would be an octopus representing something sexual.

Since Leslie is a Jungian, she would say
whether the furnace heats with oil, gas or electricity
is what's significant.

I gaze out her back window.
Gravel covers plastic sheets for a lawn,
a bathroom countertop and sink
lie upside down for the remodel.

Leslie sits in her high backed chair.

What is it? she asks.
I pull myself out of the overstuffed leather chair
and glance at her Sony tape recorder
with twin omni-directional mikes on the desk.

I am samurai. My sword sleeps under my bed
waiting for night prowlers to feel its keen edge.
My ancestors weep knowing this samurai
jogs around Greenlake wearing color-coordinated sweats,
worries about snails in the garden
and whether the dog has fleas.

Leslie's smile turns to a belly laugh,
That's a good one, she says.
Now what's really bothering you?
That World War II internment thing again?

Knot

ii

There is a knot, like a lump of coal wanting to be a diamond.
I felt it in Mrs. Waterhouse's kindergarten class
during the pledge of allegiance. My brain knew the words,
but my lips wouldn't speak because I was born an enemy of the state.

Uncle Ken's Westinghouse TV with its nine-inch black
and white screen brought the Lone Ranger, Tonto and
Victory at Sea with its haunting musical score—
black and white images of the Pacific Ocean, waves, battleships
and an enemy that looked like me.

Twenty years later our U.S. Army company of recruits
marched through Fort Polk, Louisiana. At North Fort
my buddy, McCullum, elbowed me and said, *There's your
picture, boy.*
It was an Asian face in a rice paddy with the inscription:
This is the enemy.

After my return to Seattle, I sat
in the Sunshine Café near the Space Needle,
looked at the statue of Chief Seattle,
watched as everyone was served before me.
The waitress must have known I was born
an enemy of the state.

Burial at Washelli

Mother pointed to the green canvas pavilion
where Elsie's coffin was suspended and said,
Auntie will be near your grandparents.

I remembered Elise's last New Year's party.
There were plates of teriyaki chicken, sushi,
broiled eel and the traditional New Year tai.
She recalled catching the last steamship
from Hiroshima to America before Pearl Harbor.

Her husband, Kenji, dragged out an aerial photo
of the family home at ground zero,
a barren desert of collapsed lives.
Thank God we were in Minidoka, he said.

Elsie's face was thinned by chemotherapy.
She smiled and quietly said,
Be sure to write the Archives in D.C.
to verify your internment.
Reparations are coming.

We Are Defined by Rice

In grainy black and white movies
images flicker, samurai
slay ninjas flying off rafters.

Gleefully samurai pull a rice ball
from wide sleeves like magicians,
happily feast for a week on one morsel,
almost like the revised legend of Jesus
feeding a multitude of 5,000 people
with five rice balls and two fishes.

Mother's wrinkled hands
massage tenderness and love
into each sticky grain,
a task that goes back a thousand years
before chopsticks when everything
was hands, only hands.

Our entire family goes barefoot in the surf:
cold salt water tingles and numbs.
We dance on slippery rocks
like fishermen pulling nets,
bring in each slimy wad,
black strands of seaweed.

We rinse the sand away,
dry strands on cedar slats like laundry.
Summer sea flavors
wrap winter rice balls,
crinkle and crunch,
quintessential Japanese fare.

Mother inserts pickled red plums,
Japanese ume, in the center like a heart.
White rice absorbs red juice,
her salty surprise.

Our classmates ridicule rice balls
in our lunch boxes.
Food we place at our ancestor's shrine
next to black and white photographs,
manna to nourish their spirits.

We beg Mom for yellow slices of cheese
between white bread
or peanut butter and jelly
for school lunches.

We trade away rice made with love,
summer seaweed prepared by our hands.
So easily we give ourselves away.

First Memory

Sake warmed in boiling water
like a baby's bottle in a pan
over blue flames.

Odors of Japanese cabbage,
mackerel and cigarettes descend.

Grandma and Grandpa Yamada.
In Japanese—*Ba-chan and Ji-chan*—
at home upstairs on Lane Street.

A knife clacks celery
on a wooden cutting board,
children playing, adults a pervasive whisper.

The banister, our playground,
excessive coats of white paint,
glossy enamel built up
over the years,
too tempting not to be a slide.

Quiet! Alan! Larry!
Ba-chan needs her rest.

Ba-chan began smoking
Lucky Strikes in Minidoka
purchased from the Block 33 canteen,
government supplied as consolation.
She inhaled and held the smoke
deep in her soul until it
seeped into sacred places.
She exhaled as if she would
never enjoy another.

Each exhalation a
momentary rush to forget
the Idaho desert, barbed wire,
grinding wind, and dust.

At Lane Street
my uncles gathered
in *Ba-chan*'s room:
Bob from San Francisco,
Tomokiyo from New York,
Henry from Long Island,
Shizuo from D.C.,
Kenji from Anderson Dam,
all former residents of Minidoka.

Alan chased me.
We hollered at the top of the stairs,
slid down the banister,
banged and thumped, our
six-shooter cap guns ablaze.
The battle cries and clatter of
wild cowboys and Indians.

Ba-chan passed shortly.
Mother never told me
what finally took her life.

I knew, she knew:
loud noises killed grandma.

May sounds of children playing
be my farewell.

II.

The War Years

"Herd 'em up, pack'em off and give them
the inside room of the badlands. Let'em
be pinched, hurt, hungry and dead up against it...
Personally, I hate the Japanese. And that goes
for all of them."

—Henry McLemore, a Hearst syndicated columnist for the
San Francisco Examiner, January 1942 in reference to the
relocation of the Japanese in America during World War II.

For All the Government Took

For all the government took from us
during World War II,
sixty years later I took a piece of basalt
from Minidoka, Idaho.

After the twelve hour bus ride from Seattle,
I returned to what was the Idaho desert in 1943.
Accompanied by 65 other pilgrims,
I walked the North Canal near the Snake River
where the barracks used to be.

A Park Service map marked Block 26,
temporary home of my parents during the War.
Gone were the barracks, barbed
wire, guard towers, and the 10,000 souls.

Time, nature and cultivation healed the land,
transformed the desert into green fields.
What was left—cracked concrete foundations,
crumbled masonry.

Remnants of Kubota's garden
broke through a knoll—cropping up like
ancient Druid rock formations
in the image of the eagle, wings
spread and extended,
emblazoned on the Minidoka Honor Roll
of Nisei soldiers.

The wind swirled dust clouds,
ghosts of Minidoka wandering the land.
I visualized my late father
in the Block 33 canteen,

sitting in a rocking chair,
chucking potatoes at the pot belly stove,
knocking soot loose from the pipes
on a cold Idaho morning.
I saw my mother scrub heaps
of diapers on a metal washboard.

For all the government took from us
during World War II,
sixty years later I took a piece of black basalt.

To make peace with the land,
I buried a quartz crystal,
that traveled with me
to the family grave in Hiroshima.
Pushed it deep into the soil.
Thought I heard a cry from this frozen tear.

With hands shaking, I retrieved it.
Hurled it into the canal, where
like a boulder crash, it
rippled concentric circles,
changed the course of the canal
for a minute, a day and possibly years.

A prismatic tear gazes into the desert's heart,
a tear that will never fall but will surface
in the autumn, when the North Canal is shut, will
sparkle in the dry stream bed through winter
until covered by snow, be submerged in spring
when fields are irrigated, and disappear entirely
from the waters of the Snake River
if discovered by a Minidoka pilgrim.

A souvenir from the desert
and reminder of how pain and suffering
can span lifetimes or dissipate like light fractured
into rainbows if seen through clear angles, colors
that vibrate and inhabit the soul,
power enough to release wandering ghosts
from their earthbound Minidoka.

For all that the government took from me,
I took a rock and left a crystal in its place.

Imagined President Roosevelt and the White House Cabinet Discussing the Sneak Attack on Pearl Harbor.

Here's the plan boys.
DeWitt, what you think about rounding up all
the Japanese and putting them into concentration camps
like in Germany?

We don't care if they didn't commit a crime,
and the hell with constitutional rights.
Mere stroke of the pen will do the job.
God fearing Americans will support it.

Put Italians and Germans in too?   Are you crazy?
Half of Pennsylvania and Joe DiMaggio
would be behind barbed wire.

Japanese <u>look</u> like foreigners.
Anyway it'll be for their own safety.

J. Edgar can find them, easy.
We'll send them to the ugliest, meanest desert.
Use them to build camps, just like Jesus and his cross.
Idle hands I always say...

Of course there will be barbed wire.
This isn't some East coast summer camp for rich Jewish girls.
Be sure to point the machine guns inside.
Who would want to break in?

Born farmers, them Japanese.
Turning desert into farmland will be their patriotic duty.
And when the War is over, we'll lottery off the land in chunks
to every able-bodied, white American veteran.
Call it the "Land-for-Heroes Program,"
even throw in a couple of barracks with each plot.

Helluva election year gimmick.

The War Years

The Minidoka wind whistles through
our rickety tarpaper school house.
It ruffles the gingham dress of Miss Miller
who hovers like a stone mountain.
Our white elementary teacher
with a big nose, black high-top lace shoes
and wire-framed glasses, keeps a lace hanky
tucked into one cuff.

We stand at our desks for morning inspection.
She holds a roll of toilet paper under her arm,
tears one square, dispenses each to those without hankies.
Peers into our souls through our hands, believes we are
what our hands covet: marbles, toys, and scooters.

I cherish what she teaches about liberty and justice
on the other side of the barbed wire. I imagine visiting
Miss Miller's America for one day:

> Slick back my hair and stash *The Old Man and the Sea,*
> under my coat for this adventure.
> I wear my "Lucky Lindy" leather aviator hat
> with built-in goggles, scratched lenses
> hide my slant eyes, a superhero.

> I race my wooden scooter full-tilt to town,
> whistle down the clean sidewalks of Twin Falls,
> clack–clack past the Royal Bakery—sniff their famous
> Butter Krust Bread, glide by the mannequin displays
> at Tingwalls Department Store, merrily truck to Globe Feed and Seed.
> Scrawl my name gloriously in chalk down Main Street
> like a skywriter doing loops, rescue a white Scotty injured by a car.
> Pet and hug the dog, then deliver him safely to the curb.

Wheels spin and I speed back on Hunt Road to Minidoka.
Smiling guards greet me and open the barbed wire gate gladly.
Gently pat me on the back, remind me to hurry
to the mess hall. The smell of roast turkey,
dressing and cranberry sauce entice me. Cook-san hands me
a metal food tray. I stand first in line, *The Old Man
and the Sea* under my arm, my chest puffs proudly.

This America waits beyond the wires.
I am ready now.

Enola Gay and the Big Bomb

Leaded glass fractures sunlight, bursts
into seven tinctured bands.

A son should not precede his father into night.

Prismatic faces explode and invite
vibrations that transmute a Handel Overture.
Leaded glass fractures sunlight.

Retina's lining magnetizes energy, rods excite
holographic images replicated in miniature.

A son should not precede his father into night.

Heat, flash, radiation brightness
crystallizes two eyes in rapture.
Leaded glass fractures sunlight.

An atom bomb explodes: molecules ignite—
physical bodies sundered beyond cure.
Leaded glass fractures sunlight.

A son should not precede his father into night.

Hiroshima After the War

i

Christmas chocolates set aside
for Hiroshima relatives:
See's chewy nougat, caramel-walnuts,
vanilla crème, and solid milk chocolate.

Mom convinced us to keep fruit cake—
sticky blob of candied cherries, citron,
and oranges cemented in a circular can
covered with a design of holly sprigs
and pine cones.

The tin was the only thing of value to me.
Possible home for plastic army soldiers
or mom's sewing threads and needles.

We complained to anyone
who'd listen:
all the best goes to Japan;
we got left-overs.

My brother and I believed
everyone had relatives
with homes destroyed in the War.

We hauled boxes in the Red Radio Flyer Wagon
to the Chinatown Post Office every month:

      Chocolates, coffee, medicine to trade
      on the black market, underwear
      and clothes purchased from Goodwill.
Alan and I took turns riding home.
Prevented the wagon from rattling.

50th Anniversary of the Bomb

ii

Visited Hiroshima in '95.
Met cousin Isao
who fifty years earlier
claimed our packages that
saved his family
and three sisters who
looked like mom.

Felt guilt and regret
for complaining as a child.

Chocolates and coffee traded
for rice and necessities,
medicine for cousin Akiko,
who lay trapped for days
under the rubble of the family home
1,000 meters from
ground zero.

The fallen house saved her
from becoming, as some people became,
a white outline burned onto a black cement wall—
or buried under hot ash
in mid-sentence like residents of Pompeii.

140,000 souls left this existence—
women on their way to work,
uniformed school children singing,
elderly men and women preparing morning tea—
became ghosts wandering
the purgatory of an atomic desert
before their next transformation.

Survivors became remnants,
bedraggled, soaked by radioactive rain,
guinea pigs of the first man-made mass destruction.

Akiko, a fifteen year old,
survived the blast,
heat and radiation.

Scars, like burnt islands
on a topographic map, singed
into her body, never to be revealed.
Nothing compared to
her fear of contaminating
the family line and passing
deformities to future generations.

Fear of never finding a husband—
someone to marry a woman such as she.

Sixty years later in Iraq,
U.S. troops fire bullets coated
with depleted uranium.
Scatter radioactive debris and shells,
playthings for Iraqi children.

American troops search for the Holy Grail
of nuclear death. Fear Iraqis would do
to America what we did
to Hiroshima and Nagasaki—false,
but killing us and them, all the same.

Observing from afar,
Parvati, Hindu goddess
of righteous indignation
and consort to Shiva,
furrows her brow, opens again
the blood-smeared ledger
of karmic retribution.

Hiroshima Family Grave

iii

Gray granite monument
with black Japanese script,
our family grave holds
a small drawer of ashes.
Nearby hundreds of upright markers
squeeze like a stone garden into a cemetery
bound by apartment buildings
inside the middle of the city.

Cousin Akira slides the drawer open,
maybe 1,000 years of ancestors
layered like sediment on the ocean floor.
Mentally I drill a core sample down
to the first Yamadas,
origins of my mother's family tree.
My hands want to reach into
samurai, merchants, housewives,
bomb victims and civil servants.

Maybe only 50 years of ancestors there
if the bomb converted ashes to ashes,
spread remains to the wind,
dust on the tansu, grime and pollution
precipitated from the air.

Uncle Kotaro, my mother's brother
and Japanese Navy submarine captain,
father of cousin Isao and Akiko,
died a natural death
in Hiroshima before the War.

Mom told stories of FBI men
after Pearl Harbor.
Tall white men, snappy clothes,
shiny shoes, and black fedoras
entered the grocery store,
took *Ji-chan*, her sixty-five year old father,
like a criminal by the arm, one on each side.

Mom threw her apron on the run,
caught up to the agents down the street,
fronted them, blocked boldly,
spoke with restrained venom and anger.

Kotaro, the Navy captain, my brother
died before the War.
Dad went to Japan
to bury his son
and honor his memory.
He has done nothing wrong.
You let my father go!

Mom took *Ji-chan* by the arm,
picked up her apron,
marched him unmolested
back to the store.

Rain falls into the granite box,
pock-marking the ashes.
The sound of rain on ashes,
blunted music from the sky.

I touch the stone, remember Minidoka
and my own Seattle grave under a red maple
in the Japanese section of Washelli's Cemetery
—American ghetto to ghetto.

Five cousins in blue surround me,
hold black umbrellas.
One who looks like mother,
shelters and protects me.
I gaze into my ancestors' remains.
Exhale a cleansing breath.
In this small drawer of ashes, my thoughts
return to incarnations
where I walk as a samurai
before the poisons of Minidoka
begin to flow in my veins.

Gorillas

Mom wore layers,
her best clothes,
hid the baby-bump.
Sat on her suitcase,
strapped down the bulge,
only way to bring
all she could carry.

No time to decorate the baby's room,
buy a crib, or attend a shower.
Already sold—the Baldwin piano
she loved to play in the evenings,
silverware set and never-to-be-used wedding gifts.

No idea where soldiers were taking them.
Machine guns and guard towers
surrounded the Puyallup Fair Grounds,
re-named Camp Harmony.

Lanky, blue-eyed private from Arkansas,
rifle over on his right shoulder
and bayonet fixed to his belt,
towered over a sea of black heads,
singled out mom. She said he asked:

Ya'll human beings?
You look and dress
like humans.

At the fair grounds in the decaying straw,
some unlucky Japanese bachelors
lived in animal stalls.
Barbed wire held the masses.
Food psychologically tethered them
like Pavlov's dog.

Camp Harmony, a "target rich" environment—
Japanese orphans, babies, women, children,
the infirm and able-bodied. They
must have felt their neck hairs
tingle when the machine guns swiveled
and the crosshairs hesitated.

1942 Nightmare

Kazuko, our neighbor, returns only in dreams.
On a rainy Seattle night
two black sedans park outside her apartment.
Wraiths in fedoras glide up the stairs.
My re-occurring nightmare:

>Kazuko wears her favorite pink dress. –
>smiles politely like she expects men to materialize.
>Inertia weighs heavily on me,
>I try to scream while being
>swept away in an undertow.

>I snag a shiny metal ring.
>A white-hot silver spike appears, driven deep
>into my right hand, no pain just
>the sound of crunching bones.

>From outside my body I see
>magnesium ignite in water
>as my mouth shrinks into a small red
>wound in my palm. Kazuko fades
>like a pink ghost in the mist.

Letters to her return unopened.
Police have no clues,
she appears only in dreams.
I pray the FBI, not some
all too eager others,
took her sixty years ago.

Anna's Tattoo

We stop playing when our landlord's
wild haired maid, Anna, approaches.
In spite of our fears, we don't run away
when she beckons and points
to a neat black line of many numbers
emblazoned into her olive skin,
a tattoo from German death camps—
so many numbers, so many lives.

No tattoos for Minidoka,
desert so forbidding guards cut
the barbed wire and made a clothesline.
We saw no openings,
even when they were there—
forgot freedom's scent.

Our bodies hostage, minds
twirling without a compass.

Better off tattooed,
and wear shame on our arms,
a badge, evil to curse and despise.
A reminder to transform shame to pride.
Better than hating our color,
our eyes, our innocent trust,
and only loving our country.

Hummingbird

Quicksilver messengers of the gods,
Ba-chan missed her Pacific Northwest sprites
disguised as iridescent birds. They
hovered outside her Seattle kitchen window.
Couldn't follow her to the Idaho desert.

In a dream she escaped Minidoka,
her Icarus wings disintegrated mid-air
so a hummingbird crashed to earth—
green feathers and bones blown,
then snagged in sagebrush
outside the barbed wire.

Spiders caught broken green
plumage in webs near the barrack,
a gossamer dream catcher,
organic resting place.

A feather like a stone
tipped the scale against her.

They Were Expendable

The climb was a waking nightmare –
silent ascent in moonlight,
up a 3,000 foot Italian cliff of shale.

Japanese American soldiers,
the 442 Regimental Combat Team
gripping shrubs barely rooted,
standing on rifle butts or balancing on a buddy's boot,
a high-wire act in full combat gear
—a living staircase of bones, muscle—
without a net they claw upwards
clinging to a vertical wall.

A mental lapse, a flinch—
those who fell did so silently into darkness—
a cry, a scream would reveal strategic positions.
Certain death for the entire battalion, dangling
like spiders.

Death wears many faces—
booby traps and terror with cartoon names—
screaming meemies rip the sky
and explode showering random death,
bouncing Betty mines lay down
360 degrees of shrapnel mid-air,
tear flesh but not their spirit.

Sorry to inform you letters
sent to families with names like Morihiro,
Okada, Sakamoto in American concentration camps.

Heroism was the 442's only choice.
Glory scratched out on the shoulders of comrades.
Achieved equality—color of their blood
the same as white soldiers. America's shame—
back home not one barber in Hood River, Oregon
will cut a Nisei soldier's hair.

Private First Class Harry

Ba-chan unraveled her blue sweater
as if possessed.
Ripped and salvaged yarn
to knit a hara maki,
wool wrap for her son Harry
before he shipped out to Italy.

Todd, her first son, volunteered.
Snipers at Bruyeres killed him
before she could finish his.

Knitting needles clacked furiously,
not a missed stitch or hole
for a bullet to find.

Yarn absorbed a tear, a mother's hope—
transformed wool into
a shield like chain mail. This
warm wrap, a mother's
protective surround.

Each stitch was a loop in a paper chain,
an umbilical cord that stretched to her son
six thousand miles away.

Unable to write English,
she knitted her love into blue wool,
her scent into a package of blue—
to touch her son once more.

Bainbridge Island, Washington—They Were the First

Eagle Harbor ferry pier, where
aromatic creosote oozed down
black barnacle-covered pilings,
swayed and rocked rhythmically
with each wave.

Fragrance of Puget Sound's
green salt water:
rich with brown foam, kelp,
seaweed and driftwood.

Silver perch glide past the dock,
nibble mussels clustered on pilings.
Red-orange rock-crabs and starfish
glow iridescent in the shallows.

Seagulls squawk above,
harass a lone bald eagle mid-air,
snipe at tail feathers.

*

Ji-chan cleared land,
felled cedars and pines
in rain, fog and mist
of Pacific Northwest winters.
Dynamited stumps,
explosions swallowed by the forest.

Horses hauled timber
to a clearing near the red barn.
Firewood stacked neatly,
protected with canvas.

His bonfire crackled,
ignited scrub and twisted branches
into glowing embers
carried by the winds.

Ji-chan tended the fire, cleared land,
hunted pheasants and chased
varmints from the chicken coop,
with the pop-pop of his .22 rifle.

Snow-covered Mount Olympus
stood west of the clearing.
When wind blew from the southeast,
he said he could feel on the back of his neck
the glaciers of Mount Rainier
100 miles across Puget Sound.

Spirits of earth
returned his love and care.
Strawberries thrived
in bounty during short summers.

*

Bainbridge supplied
America with berries,
sweet and fragrant—
graced Queen Victoria's table
with their plump presence
during her Canadian visit.

Strawberry harvest festival,
pride of the Community,
Japanese girls in silk kimonos rode
decorated farm trucks on parade
beside their white classmates,
almost equals.

Ferries with Indian names,
Kehlohken and Klickitat,
carried berry crops to Seattle,
loaded on trains, taken to market.

*

After Pearl Harbor, black
fastback sedans caravanned
from Seattle in 1942,
rumbled off the ferries,
across the wooden pier planks, then
scattered over the Island
like a motorized octopus with tentacles,
enclosing one woman and
thirty-three Japanese men
including *Ji-chan.*

FBI confiscates his dynamite
for blasting stumps,
.22 caliber varmint hunting rifle,
Motorola radio and binoculars.

Black fastbacks head to ferry docks
like a gust of ill wind.
Ji-chan taken to where
he will never smell the sea,
feel the glaciers of Rainier,
plow straight rows,
see loved ones for years.

*

Two months later hundreds of Japanese
shuffle onto the planks
of the Eagle Harbor pier.

In a photo, older brother Frank
cradles his toy John Deere tractor,
Mom grabs Frank's hand.
Government identity tags
pinned to coats with family names
and numbers, flap like windsocks.

On-lookers and well-wishers watch
Bainbridge Island Japanese,
first to be evacuated in the nation,
parade down the pier,
in their Sunday best
with only possessions
they can carry.

Pets left with neighbors,
strawberry fields untended,
school classrooms half empty.

Armed guards escort
Japanese to the Kehlohken ferry,
to Seattle. Herded then onto trains
at Colman dock, black-out
curtains echo all the way to Bergen Belsun.

Curious on-lookers
photograph images of
Japanese looking so well dressed,
No one waves goodbye.

Molly, Frank's dog,
refuses to eat,
cries every night, runs away.
Someone says they spotted
her waiting near the Eagle Harbor pier.

Weeks before the evacuation,
Kouras, Nakatas and other families
picnicked near Eagle harbor,
waded into the icy waters.
Raked clams and snails from rocks,
boiled treasures in salt water
over a fire on the beach.

As kids, we pried
hard snail feet off with a pin,
eagerly devoured the sweet innards
that tasted like the sea.
Ba-chan unpacked *bento*:
rice balls, sushi, strawberries, hot tea
and teriyaki chicken.
Winds sprinkled rice balls with sand,
our kid-favorite—orange soda pop and rice balls—
with sand.

*

Gradually after the War all Issei *ji-chan*s
and *ba-chans* passed away,
some in camp, others after returning.
Frank graduated, married, became a father
and is now a *ji-chan* with grandchildren.

Koura and Sons Farm—
once 190 acres, home of sweet Marshall strawberries
where grandkids rode their bikes
with abandon and freedom—
a golf course after the War
with *no trespassing* signs.

Frank, as a *ji-chan*,
adopts a dog named Molly
at an animal shelter,
a ferry boat ride away
from that misty island.

Winter whiteness sweeps
across Bainbridge,
softly covers sharp edges.
Cleanses the heart,
quiets anger.
Rekindles our desire to work the land,
give our children things
we once could not even imagine.

We watch our children
build driftwood bonfires,
rake clams and dart among
cedar shadows like forest sprites.
Listen to them laugh
and play tag after a red sun descends
behind the witnessing Olympic Mountains.

Black Hole

The world turns gently
in this recurring nightmare.
Trees and flowers surround me,
circling faster and faster,
now a whirlwind.

I know this dream, I say.

The hospital bed spins,
I am frozen and immobile,
fight to place a foot on the floor,
but vertigo rules.
I pull off the oxygen mask
and rip the IVs .
The tubes dangle.

I say my dying words,
Minidoka, be damned,
and wake.

Minidoka, Idaho is
a black hole,
where gravity pulls light in
and nothing comes out.

I recall how the Minidoka Japanese wept
for the loss of sons and
daughters fighting for America,
remembered relatives and friends incinerated
in Hiroshima, Nagasaki, Okinawa
and the Tokyo fire bombings—
a half million names, faces, souls.

Under the Idaho night sky
with constellations aglow,
500,000 Japanese names
written among a glaze of clouds
hovering low.

*

Sixty years have passed.
The irrigated desert is green,
barracks are farmhouses and sheds.
Guard towers and machine guns
have not survived the years.

These night stars and constellations—
sparkling then, sparkling now.
Japanese must have looked
to other worlds and galaxies
beyond the Milky Way,
above the pull of Minidoka.

For pilgrims this is not
where the sick and infirm
rejoice and leave their crutches in heaps.

I seek forgiveness here
for crimes I did not commit,
and redemption for being Japanese
during a time of war.

Still, when I step
into the black hole
it fails to swallow me up.
Strength from all those who perished—
that Hiroshima burning mass anchors,
nourishes my resolve to walk with dignity
as one man in two worlds.

Go Game

Go board inscription reads:
T.K. Yamada, Minidoka, Ida., Dec. 25, 1944,
Christmas gift after release from FBI camps.

Ji-chan never talks about the board,
only the game of infinite possibilities.
He is a master of clicks and grunts—
game stones snap loudly, fiercely.

He sips green tea,
glances at the sushi plate,
cradles the wooden bowl
of black slate game pieces.

He withdraws a flat circular stone
between his right index and middle finger,
Raises it above his head,
vigorously arcs it to the board,
an intimidating click,
followed by a grunt of satisfaction.

Men speak Japanese on the porch,
chant and sing, conduct New Year rituals,
invite *Ji-chan* to join—
grunt and throw down mallets in rhythm,
thump rice into ambrosia.

The soul of Japanese people

transplanted in America,
gohan pounded rhythmically
on the community granite stone.

Crowds gather around
men, elastic in their motions
like gandy dancers pounding spikes
for the Northern Pacific.

Wooden mallets clack.
Mr. Ito's deft hands
dart and turn the steaming
gohan, sprinkle water
in that interval before the mallet strikes.

Thumps and slaps transform
gohan into *mochi*,
a gooey white blob,
for the New Year's Day's feast.

Ji-chan and his friends sit
cross-legged in the living room
just below the cigar smoke haze,
continue ancient game of possession
and possibilities.

His emotions, denied during internment,
emerge like sharp knives positioned
on a board carved with his name.
Decades of silence: *gaman*, the Japanese way,
to endure the unbearable with dignity.

Unlike previous 1,000 game moves,
this snap rips the air.
Crisp and sharp, it echoes around the room,
bounces, dissipates in smoke as if alive.

Ji-chan's stoic façade shows stress
as mallets clack granite,
he exhales a grunt so forbidding,
it almost transforms *gohan* into *mochi*.
But before the last mallet strikes, pain
turns to silence.

III.

No Longer Heroes

"As children growing up in the 1950s we watched 'Victory at Sea' on television. It had a beautiful Richard Rogers musical score that was as haunting as waves rolling in the Pacific....We cheered for the victorious Americans and winced because the enemy looked like us."

—from *Community and Difference: Teaching, Pluralism and Social Justice* edited by Roberto A. Pena, Kristin Guest, and Lawrence Y. Matsuda

Roots—Lt. Ehren Watada

i

> Death, even at one's own hands, is believed
> to be the highest evolution of a samurai.

Nisei soldiers, most decorated unit
in American military history:
Go for Broke—their motto,
the Hawaiian dice player's slogan
for shoot the works,
everything on the line.

Fatigue that drains resolve
and turns the bravest into cowards,
is ignored by modern samurai.
Hunger and losses only fuel
the desire to prove loyalty.
They claw and scratch uphill,
take more casualties than
"Texas Lost Battalion" soldiers
they rescue.

Victory means puncturing the German
Gothic Line of defense.
Ignoring the irony of loved ones
suffering behind American barbed wire,
Nisei liberate Jews in Dachau.
The highest evolution of a soldier,
placing country above self.

U.S. Senator Daniel K. Inouye,
while running for office,
has his loyalty questioned.
He raises his empty sleeve,
his right arm given for democracy in Italy.
He would sacrifice the other gladly.
Becomes a politician, next highest evolution.

Court Martial of Lt. Ehren Watada

ii

Refused deployment to Iraq.

Ehren: are you the next step in evolution?
Fish that leaps out of military muck,
breathes fresh air, evolves into Gandhi
of army officers, protests war.

Or are you U.S. Warrant Officer
Hugh Thompson, reborn as a Japanese?
Maneuvers OH-23 chopper at My Lai
between Charlie company troops who are
killing, sodomizing and raping.
Thompson orders his gunners
to shoot Americans if the slaughter continues,
demands officers stop or die.

He pulls survivors from a ditch
used as mass grave. Drags out
a small crimson drenched boy.
Evacuates survivors and calls in two gun ships,
medevacs twelve civilians.

Thompson's reward for invoking
personal values in battle:
increasingly dangerous missions,
crashes five times, broken back.
Recovers to witness all
who murder the villagers
set free, one by President Nixon.

Your quest, Ehren Watada, is to become
a moral beacon in an America

that loves Superbowl Sunday,
and stories of Anna Nicole's premature death.
You give up your career, rescind your oath
and choose jail—just another
sad story without legs, not sexy.
Moral army officers should have
a press agent instead of high priced lawyers

who require more than lieutenant's pay
and public pleas for money.

Go for broke and sell your memoirs.
Start a charity to feed Iraqi orphans.
Become next highest evolution,
something the masses will appreciate.

I recall a chess game,
vicious war of attrition.
On a half empty game board,
I push a pawn past danger and death,
turn it into royalty:
the next highest evolution of a soldier,
one who puts down his sword
when to strike is
to demean the soul.

Blaine Methodist Church Presentation

iii

Ehren Watada should have fallen
quietly on his *katana*
like a masterless samurai.

He rubs his eyes red,
folds his arms,
lowers his head for a moment,
sighs and glances at his girlfriend and father.
Resumes an erect posture for the presentation.

Ehren traded steel swords
for a blade of bamboo,
unfit to commit hara kiri
and disembowel himself.

Some in the audience whisper,
"Death to traitors and cowards."
They would gladly serve as his second,
lift their swords, sever his head,
and complete the ritual,
then cleanse their blades
with water trickled over
the sword's scrolling temper-line,
wiped dry with a sheet of white paper.

Ehren asks, *What if our elected leaders become the enemy?*
Calls on all soldiers to lay down their weapons.
He breaks ranks to save lives
and prevent more from dying in an illegal war.

His bamboo sword is
a reminder to all
citizens in a democracy
that we are responsible
for needless deaths.

I remember, a Buddhist monk from Hokkaido
who preached about mindful living—
how all Japanese are connected:
to that prehistoric grain of rice
emerging from a bog,
to the first time a *bachan*
pressed red pickled plums
into the heart of a steaming rice ball,
or how the sound of a warrior's first slash
cuts through a nation.

I understand now as if it were
my own choice, why Ehren Watada
put down the swords
of death, why no harm
can come to the enlightened,
and how a future Buddha emerges
like a white lotus from a stagnant pond.

FBI After 9-11

Divided worlds twist, then intersect, crash
like a head-on car wreck.
FBI invade a California Muslim home, surround the family.
A piercing cry for mercy from a daughter
in a designer blouse
and jeans, sequined jacket ripped
to gain submission.

Archetypal Jungian images collide,
child verses insect-faced men
with visors down, black flak jackets
that scrunch and squeak like new leather,
automatic weapons at the ready,
microcosm of *War on Terror*.

Another time, another place
the solution would be medieval,
unspeakable acts visited on
worshipers of the wrong god, those
given the fast lane to hell.

The terrified girl screams,

Let mother cover her face
in the presence of men.

Bodies quiver, tension mounts,
a pistol at her head. Everyone
unsure of what should happen next.

She won't stop screaming,
because she can't understand
why they don't understand.
They see her tears but never grasp
how an uncovered female face
could be a sin.

War on Terror—Border Crossing

U.S. border guards peer through
reflective sunglasses, pull me out of line.
I see them as Block 26 guards
from the Minidoka concentration camp
sixty years ago.

In camp, many Nisei tried to be 110% Americans—
fought against Hitler, bought war bonds, labored
in munitions factories. After the War,
some changed their last names,
turned white on paper,
"Takahashi" to "Highbridge", the English translation.

I remove my dark glasses;
explain my purpose;
joke about not drinking the water.

My manner and striped bowtie
do not exempt me from
being treated like an illegal alien.
No illusions about my place
as a lesser American,
but I won't shuffle my feet for them—instead
stoically accept this delay
and bottle my anger like my parents at Minidoka.
My brief public humiliation
shows all who pass how safe America is,
same way Minidoka protected:
corralling the fear.

I carry my own fence.
Barbed wire encircles me always.
Determined not to follow my parents' path
into clinical depression or a bleeding ulcer—
my shins are raked by the steel teeth
of my unwilled confinements.
Wearing this yellow skin, I am unable
to walk freely in my own country.
But I learn, border by border,
to leap safely in sudden movements
leaving no remnants snagged on the wire.

Daruma Maker

Daruma, a Japanese symbol,
for resilience, resembles an egg, a pear.
Hollow within and heavy on the bottom,
doll that tips but never stays down.
Fall down seven times, get up eight.

Darumas are blind at inception.
Blindness manifests and transforms.
A dot for an eye begins the wish.
Destruction must follow when two eyes appear
and the wish is granted.

A thousand *Darumas* populate
Uncle Tomokiyo's wooden shrine
which occupies half his living room.
Crowded on shelves like
spent nuclear rods, hollow pieces of art
await the next transformation.

With his MAC System-9 he deletes, transfigures,
cuts and pastes—virtual darumas pour out.
Red and blue creatures with and without moustaches
explode onto the color monitor,
templates to be shaped.

His one thousand *darumas* await the fire,
the next transformation, fraction of the 210,000
obliterated in Hiroshima and Nagasaki.

I remember the Hiroshima Peace Memorial Museum—
photos of burnt flesh, keloid scars, charred bodies frozen
in fetal positions, and a brown hair wad
from a victim's head on display.

Those who choose life in this wasteland
rise once more like my *daruma*
after its headfirst fall off the dining room table—
only to vibrate back and forth
progressively, lurch to a stop
and stand up promptly.

My Hiroshima relatives are *darumas* dressed in blue
suits and dresses. How proud and straight
they stand as they greet me, bowing, pumping my hand—
on the 50th anniversary of the bomb
until I am bobbing upright
stabilizing at last in their steady embrace.

In Memory of Cliff

for Cliff Barda and Sue Tomita

Cliff was the Jewish son of an Egyptian
stage-door Johnny and a red haired American cabaret
singer in Paris before World War II.

Cliff's funeral photo burned
at the Tibetan Buddhist altar at temple.
His bright smile transported
his image, curled,
then crumbled to ashes.

This was a second marriage for both
as they neared retirement.
He passed so quickly.   Their vows said in March,
he was buried in May.
Cliff loved his wife, Sue, more dearly
than his imported collapsible bicycle
he rode across town from Northgate
to the Fauntleroy ferry
up to the Vashon Island house on the hill.

Recovered from cancer surgery and
a heart operation, he proudly showed off
a scar that ran down his chest and forked
into an upside down "Y".
A Japanese sign to get married soon.

Banzai! We cheered toasting the newlyweds,
may you live a thousand years.
Cliff required two blood transfusions,
last shot of life before he said, *I do*.

Sue, her grown son, Jason, and his wife,
with Cliff's two daughters gathered
at his hospital bed two months later
to celebrate his birthday,
joined hands when he passed
and sang Happy Birthday to a silent Cliff.

Grief binds the soul to the earth.
They sang. They kept on singing.

Salmon Dreams

A river
swollen with
spawned-out Kings.
Carcasses rock
gently in the shallows.
Fingerlings, sustained,
head downstream
nourished for the trip.

The river
boils over
a deer carcass
across a submerged tree.
Hooves flap aimlessly.

The spirits of the water call.
My son holds a silver urn.
Scatters my ashes in Alaska
on the Kenai River where
I caught my first King
and where one day I become
a fish, a river, and an ocean.

Sun Ya Bar

The rising sun transforms
Roger Shimomura like a Japanese Clark Kent
into Superman—this professor emeritus,
internationally known painter,
direct descendant of castle samurai,
and master of illusion.

Roger's drawings: densely packed
over-lapping images of samurai,
kabuki actors' grimacing faces,
rice cookers, jet planes, caricatures
of Asians, Warhol-like Marilyns,
Superman in various stages
of undress, barbed wire,
guard towers, chopsticks held by disembodied hands,
and cheek to cheek geishas.
In the chaos, sometimes Roger's face appears.

Sun Ya is Roger's evening haunt.
Obeying a primordial call,
Roger climbs into his Chevy Astro Van.
He tosses his laptop into the front seat
and migrates to another existence—
dark depths of Seattle's Chinatown,
the Sun Ya Bar.

Stiff singe of Chevas Regal
and Chinese food intermingle
with cigarette smoke, create a mist,
a fog that floats across the ceiling,
floor and walls, that leaves
a fine film on the bar like a snail track
glistening on cement.

Years from now an archaeologist
will peel away layers of residue
and find this moment: when Roger
clicks on his grandmother's diaries
in his laptop and writes,
Honor demands retribution.

Under the luminous glow of the big screen TV,
five Shimomura samurai cross over,
a proud line of forty generations,
demand the warrior's life from their progeny,
and retribution for detention camps,
firebombing of Tokyo—
Roger's ancestral home.

Retribution for the hundreds of thousands
of souls incinerated at Hiroshima and Nagasaki.
Roger wields a paintbrush deftly,
his weapon of choice,
taking care to maintain the lines,
the separation of colors, slashing open
old racial wounds with a stroke:
the stereotypes, prejudice and shame.

Pencil drawings of the Minidoka desert
evoke: clouds of internment,
miscegenation laws,
false shame of difference.

Bushido, warrior's code of honor,
demands retribution
from this master-less samurai
in paint-blotched clothes.
Roger's canvases erupt with images that belie

white American stereotypes of Japanese
and overcome stigma of epicanthic folds.

Inspired by his grandmother's Minidoka diaries,
a fortress of healing emerges,
jolts sleepwalkers from a miasma.
The red, white and blue flies behind barbed wire.
Like a surgeon he re-sets shattered bones
until colors and blood stain his shirt.

Sometimes amid
the chaos and anger,
his smiling face appears.

Higo's Five and Dime

My mother tows me in the red
Radio Flyer to Higo's in Japantown
when the Smith Tower looms tallest
west of the Mississippi
and sidewalks on Jackson Street
are knotty planks.
I drop pebbles between sidewalk cracks.
Imagine them tumbling to China.

Shopkeeper bells chime our arrival.
A silk kimono from "Occupied Japan"
drapes a blond mannequin.
The family dog curls near the cash register
and beside it, wind-up toys.

Back room curtains slide open and Matsuyo,
the family matriarch, emerges wearing an apron.
Her grey hair is pulled into a bun. She
smiles like Eleanor Roosevelt, all teeth.

Kawaii ne, she greets me, "cute" in Japanese.
Opens a box of *Tomoe Ame* candy,
carefully extracts one square chunk of sweetness
wrapped in translucent rice paper,
hands me the prized morsel.

Before the War, Chiyoko, her second daughter,
succumbs quietly to tuberculosis upstairs.
Matsuyo draws the blinds,
unwraps a bar of Ivory soap, dips
a sponge in warm water,
and bathes her daughter's body.
She fixes Chiyo's hair in a French Roll,
dresses her in white for the mortuary.

Sanzo, Matsuyo's husband, dies after
their return from Minidoka,
when *Made in Japan* means cheap and shoddy
and Issei are forbidden to become US citizens.

The Japanese community is broken.
Sento bath houses stand silent, toy prizes disappear
from *Tomoe Ame* boxes and Japanese flee
to suburban split level homes and strip malls.

For decades the family waxes the linoleum floors
and prepares meals in the backroom
next to the family shrine.

Sanzo's dream of a family business
that mends the community
survives to a time when
Made in Japan means quality,
sidewalks of Jackson Street are concrete,
pebbles stop falling to China.

Green tea leaves steep in the backroom
when Sanzo beckons.
Matsuyo rises, apron in hand—
slides the curtain for the final time.

Shopkeeper bells chime, the sound lingers
then fades. The Higo legacy passes to
Ayako, Kazuichi, Masako,
Paul, and now John and Binko-san.

Five and dime memorabilia
sparkle next to arts and crafts.
Higo evolves into the Kobo Gallery,

magnet for a community dispersed.
It is a vortex where togetherness binds us as family.
I find sanctuary and peace among the hive of memories.
Cup my hands like a child,
catch and savor the sweet morsels of acceptance.

No Longer Heroes

I said a prayer for New Orleans
remembering my last trip to the Big Easy.
Morning streetlights cast an eerie pall,
that year, before Hurricane Katrina.

The Royal Orleans Hotel windows fogged
and wept, something to do
with humidity. My hand wiped a space
in the glass and saw Captain Lou
rumbling his Chevy truck
down St. Louis Street trailering a jet sled
for my Mississippi bayou fishing experience.

Pulled into the landing at Lafitte,
a small river town founded
by descendents of Jean Lafitte, the pirate.

Twin Honda outboards thundered and
pressed air heavy against my chest.
The sun rose orange and laid down
flames reflecting on the river—
crescendo into a red dawn.

Our wake dissipated,
harmlessly bumping shrimp boats
dropping nets and floats.

Katrina destroyed Lafitte
and gave the world countless primetime
hours of suffering and pain to witness.

Americans, abandoned like third-world refugees,
confused and starving at the Superdome.
Images of looters with shopping carts at Walmart
next to policemen loading baskets with shoes.

Victims are stranded on rooftops for days,
abandoned dogs whine, firefights and
lawlessness erupt in the Superdome.

Where is John Wayne on the beach
with amphibious landing craft, soldiers,
tanks, and earth movers?

Where is Jimmy Stewart on a soapbox
in the Superdome stammering inspirational
words to entranced masses?

Flood waters rise to the White House,
wash up the FEMA director like
flotsam on the world stage.

Back home the oldies station plays "American Pie".
We were heroes, I think, *before the music died.*

Reflections While Falling

I observe a young Asian woman
protecting her modesty as a breeze gusts.
She quells the uprising
of her billowing pleated skirt
with the Seattle Times.
It reads:

The Cascadia subduction zone slipped,
and Vancouver Island moved 0.14 inches
to the west yesterday.

I extend my arms,
anticipate a four point landing
and a belly-flop on concrete.

Fourteen days could bring the Big One,
something to challenge Hurricane Katrina
and the submerging of New Orleans.

Mindful of my earthbound condition
and the law of gravity,
I recall that Marilyn Monroe,
even in the gravest wind,
never wore a slip
or used a newspaper to keep down
the flare of her thighs
in the *Seven Year Itch.*

Above the subway grate,
her pleated dress mushrooms in the air;
she smiles and happily fights
a losing battle to hold the skirt down.

Concrete digs into my palms,
peels skin and scrapes gaps
in my lifeline.

A gust of wind billows from me.
My knees skid and the palms that kept
my face from being skinned
swell like pregnant Mount Saint Helens
building her lava dome
four meters a day.

Fourteen days could bring the big one.
Sirens will blare again in Kelso
when Saint Helens blows tons
of mountain, ripping out
a highway of rock, mud and trees.
Safety is the high ground.

With the world spinning,
gravity pulling, oceans warming,
subduction zones slipping,
mountains rising, skirts flaring
and hurricanes blasting—
how's a guy supposed to cross a street?

Survivor

The grass steamed that August morning when
Dad handed me a hatchet and said,
Time you killed something, boy.

Odor of chicken manure clawed up my nostrils.
I dragged open the wire gate
and snagged a brown hen, wings flapping,
a scream stuck in her throat.

I whirled the bird over my head to make her dizzy, like
I'd seen my father do, slammed her onto the block,
aimed for the neck, missed and whipped
the axe down on her beak.

Dad found me with shreds of chicken locked in my hands
and my face pocked hollow with blood.

Five years later, when I was sixteen
the neurosurgeon gave my father a year to live.
Mom wept and asked, *What shall we do?*
I added our monthly bills,
subtracted my check for working
twenty-four hours a week at Food Giant
and Mom's sewing money,
came up a hundred dollars short.

I scanned our one-bedroom apartment like a sailor
in an overcrowded lifeboat.
Saw brown linoleum floors, the Murphy bed
and the sofa where my brother slept.
I lied and said, *Ma everything will be okay.*

Dad survived,
became a grandfather,
watched my five year old son, Matthew
climb the jungle gym,
fall, bounce to the Astroturf. He
wiped his grandson's tears away.

Later we three sat bare-footed
on Matthew's bunk-bed singing
Old Macdonald had a farm,
casting lines into a make-believe sea
waiting for the wily fuzz-ball to bite.

Finding Morelia, Michoacan.de Ocampo

for Alfredo Arreguin

Wine glasses purple to the brim
sooth the restless soul.
Alfredo no longer the aspiring artist who
swings on Blue Moon Tavern chandeliers.

Tonight he holds court,
remembers his childhood trip
with his grandfather
to Morelia, Michoacán.

Family, he says, *means more than fame.*

His English words ripe—
smooth and luscious,
in their Mexican precision
launch like fireworks: skyrocket
to the ceiling, explode into ever-expanding
bursts of colors, then cascade as embers.

Alfredo recalls peering through train windows
beyond clouds of sooty smoke that yield
to a lush countryside, purple mountains.
Thick forests and billowing seas of dried grass
emerge. Pintos gallop with abandon
to the chunking rhythm of the train from Morelia,
place of his birth, home of Conquistadors.

A majestic city glows golden in his paintings,
surrounded by green jungles teeming
with red-orange toucans
and yellow-eyed jaguars.

Alfredo dances barefooted in the town square,
l'enfant terrible, a fatherless orphan of love.

Love means more than fame.

Morelia becomes a dream,
an imaginary place

only children remember
and adults never find.

Memories materialize on canvas:
thin contours, shape-lines,
filled in with layers of brilliant colors
trap thousands of pulsating
swirls, ovals and hidden faces.
Every molecule sparkles
as if held in the Madonna's arms.

His blue eyes explained in Mexico City:
eyes of the Conquistador set in Alfredo's Michoacan face—
his blue-eyed father, appears
to claim his son and embrace his art.

Absorbed by his paintings,
falling through their looking glass,
his testimony, his cauldron—colors
envelop, transform me
into a blue-eyed child. Like him
I search for that protected
place of belonging where ripe
mango clusters grow iridescent.
Where fathers embrace their sons.

Listening to his story of reconciliation,
the love of his lost father—
the mental shackles of my internment shatter
into a thousand coral snakes
twisting on the ground.

I kick them aside like a wild pinto
and sprint through frothy waves
of green to the golden heart, Morelia,
cradled between purple mountains.

Alfredo, descent of conquistadors and Indians,
chases schools of spawning King Salmon with me, the samurai.
Adventure is our compass to the essence of all living things.
We scale the white claw-shaped crests
of Hokusai's blue tsunami waves,
descend into troughs and rise above Fujii,
the eternal mountain.

Salmon Journey

for Tess Gallagher and Raymond Carver

Fishing rods destined
for the Port Angeles museum
lean in a corner
by Tess's front foyer.
Silver herring scales
stick to cork handles
as if held in loving hands yesterday.

Twenty years ago she and Ray
pull out of Port Angeles
for their last fishing trip into
the Strait of Juan DeFuca.

Framed photo on the kitchen wall
captures that day when
human beings pose with six Chinook
brothers on the dock.

Lucky on the water
and in life, instinctively they
seek that sweet spot
where time and space
converge as fate takes up their lines.
Baits sink into green depths,
head for the magical intersection
that connects to primordial energies.

Today I wash the black granite
of Ray's grave on a cliff
that overlooks the Strait
of Juan DeFuca, Tess stands
beside me and arranges

a bed of rocks and oyster shells on stone,
places purple Mums by his side.

She writes a note of love in a book
housed in a metal box
next to his grave.

Her life a reminder that
time and death are meaningless
in this place of illumination.
Rapture and transcendence
of all things are with her daily.
She holds this stillness and
dissolves into Salmon
at the end of Ray's line,
rises as mist, Mother goddess,
smoke in a cedar long house.

She lends me Ray's rod and reel
and says, *Much luck stored here.*
Tess advises me to take a life with honor,
praise the fight, enjoy the flesh, and tell the story.
I merge with the eternal cycle,
a mystical union that feeds my spirit
and spawns myths
to nourish a starving society.

Below the cemetery are green
waters of Juan DeFuca.
Little time left to fish,
before the museum claims the rod.

Matsutake Tori—The Last Pine Mushroom Hunt

Slices of *matsutake*
simmer in a broth of bonito flakes,
green scallions,
essence of the pine forest in autumn.

Family secrets pass:
how sunlight patterns the forest floor
how the rains sift through boughs
to nourish the mossy lumps
that hide *matsutake*.

Chanterelles for white people,
red mushrooms for Italians,
but we pick only light gold colored matsutake.

Two walking sticks support Dad
as he navigates the mossy hills.
He rests on a knoll and whispers,
Under that log, last year I found three.

Silver Spring campgrounds near Mount Rainier.
Generations came here:
my grandfather, my father—
me, with my son as a child.

Lunch is cold somen noodles
and steaming hot broth.
Dad fills the empty thermos with
fresh spring water.

On the return home
past Lake Wilderness Lodge,
he nods in the back seat, then murmurs:

For a while before the War
they let Japanese have dance parties here.

Dad and Mom dance
the Swing until the evacuation.

Pregnant in Minidoka, she
wears her orange summer dress.
She is round, like the full moon aglow,
Mount Rainier-ice cream cone round.

Possessed by radio music
from a nearby barrack,
she waltzes alone after dusk.
Sashays near the barbed wire,
undulates with my brother floating
in amniotic fluid, kicking rhythmically
to music from the Crystal Ballroom.

She is just another wonder of nature
like ripe pears, apples and pumpkins,
growing large in the summer heat.

She remembers the fragrance of *matsutake*,
and blossoms. At dusk she exudes a
Northwest forest perfume that coaxes
the Idaho honey bees from their silver cedar hives
for one last nightcap.

Arc de Triomphe, 2003 Invasion of Iraq

for Karen

Two-tone Parisian sirens blare
across the Seine,
trumpet the American war in Iraq.

I emerge from the Metro.
Sunlight shining
on red newsstand headlines,
Irak, C'est la Guerre.

I speak broken French,
chat in Japanese,
whisper in English,
an easy disguise
for one born in Minidoka.

One hundred motorcycles
circle the Right Bank,
relentless phalanx
holds Rue de Rivoli hostage.
Thunder hammers the pavement,
shakes the massive cleaning balls
that once rammed
down sewers combating Black Death,
rattling the bones of six million
shelved like volumes
of a dusty human library
in the catacombs.

La Marseillaise, a patriotic call to arms,
stirs spirits from subterranean Paris,
like the Arc de Triomphe
surfacing in a sea of honking taxis.

Winged Victory with a gaping mouth,
furies atop her head, sword in hand,
exhorts volunteers to glory.

I am an American Odysseus
tempted by sirens—for a moment I resist
raising my fist against America, against war. Then

remember Minidoka barbed wire and Idaho desert.
Cinch a red bandana around my forehead.

My short gray hair no longer
falls black to shoulders.
Spirits draw me into this Parisian riptide.
I am one of many boiling
and churning in a river
of humanity marching
the Right Bank chanting:

> *Paris contre la guerre.*
> *Paris contre la guerre.*

I stand for the old America,
home of the Japanese-American
442 purple heart battalion,
that wins fame as the wedge
that drives through Nazi lines.

I become an ex-patriot,
follow Richard Wright, James Baldwin,
and Langston Hughes.
Bathe under a golden waterfall
of liberty and fraternity
in the shadow of Notre Dame.
Luxuriate in Parisian canyons

near the Champs Elysee.
Shed my skin like an underwater
snake at the Moulin Rouge.
Watch the translucent membrane
flutter into the chanting crowd
to the sewers of Paris.

Without this inflexion of skin, my eyes
fall away from their sockets
as in the catacombs.

I wake like a dreamer
from slumber and see
the world through Monet and Degas.

I am a pond of deep blue,
a shimmering ballet dancer.
I am the Winged Victory with furies
shouting to my fellow marchers:

En Amerique, Je suis Japonais.
En Paris, Je suis Americain
contre la guerre.

Afterword—Comments and Observations
—Dr. Tetsuden (Tetsu) Kashima

Various issues were common to all ten WRA centers. For example, the WRA Administrative Manual became the handbook for center procedures and operations. It detailed the method of internal police activity, newspaper policy, leave clearance, acceptable and unacceptable conduct, and numerous other necessary procedures to maintain daily life for the thousands of men, women and children held in a limited, bounded, and militarily secured area. Other common all-center actions resulted in considerable hardships, anxiety, disruptions, and controversy. For example, the earlier mentioned "Loyalty Questionnaire," asked Nisei adult males whether they would be willing to serve in the armed forces wherever ordered. A number of Nisei responded by saying that they would be willing to do so as soon as their parents were released. This response was viewed as a "qualified" answer and usually resulted in his transfer to the Tule Lake Segregation Center. Another universal issue later dealt with the military draft of eligible Nisei males from January to August 1944. The Army sent WRA camps, 2,213 draft physical notices and while the majority of the Nisei complied, 267 refused to report and 91 others later refused to be inducted. In his dismissal of the indictment against twenty-seven Tule Lake Segregation Camp Nisei who refused the draft notice, U.S.

district court judge, Louis Goodman, in July 1944, stated that, "It is shocking to the conscience that an American citizen be confined on the grounds of disloyalty and then, while so under duress and restraint, be compelled to serve in the armed forces or be prosecuted for not yielding to such compulsion."barbed wire concentration camp."[5]

Other instances revolved around the conduct of the omnipresent military guards at each WRA center. By wars end, the guards had shot and killed four persons, all of whom were innocent and unarmed. Other issues, although seemingly less dramatic, nevertheless required the incarcerated to take notice and adjust to such intrusions into their lives that were never part of their pre-Center existence. These included the lack of privacy, especially for the women forced to suffer the use of a common Army-style latrine facility. Indignities included the inclusion of animal organs such as sweetbread and liver which many incarcerated Buddhists found religiously unacceptable as meal-time entrees. There was also the break-down of family unity and discipline as the WRA systematically discredited the Issei pre-War Japanese values and attempted to inculcate American middle-class values and norms such as egalitarianism and Americanization. A common reaction by the adult incarcerated included ennui and anxiety about an unknown future they were forced to endure while suffering an enforced idleness for a group known for their diligent and productive work-ethic. Insensitive and occasionally hostile WRA administration, military guards, and Justice Department official actions resulted in flash points of overt resentment, anger, and reciprocated suspicion from the incarcerated to the incarcerator.

Notably, in Hawaii, with a population of 150,000 persons of Japanese ancestry there was no mass exclusion

5. Muller, Eric, *Free to Die for Their Country*, Chicago: University of Chicago Press, 2003.15

and incarceration. When the call went out for volunteers to join a segregated Army unit in early 1943, there was an overwhelming rush to volunteer such that the Army ran out of typewriters to keep up with the paperwork to process the responses.[6] The reactions from the WRA centers hardly necessitated any typewriters to process the volunteer forms. In Hawaii, the entire disposition from the military, government officials and political leaders to persons of Japanese ancestry was one of inclusion for all to work toward the allied victory; in the West Coast, the characterization was one of exclusion and, to stigmatize a group solely on their ancestry.

---

6. Tom Coffman, The First Battle: the Battle for Equality in War-Time Hawaii, Honolulu: Hawai'i Council for the Humanities, 2007, video.

Final Comments on *A Cold Wind From Idaho*

In the hauntingly poignant poems in this volume, Larry Matsuda, leads the reader from the pre-1942 incarceration days through the devastating wasteful years in the primitive barbed wire prison enclosures, out to the hopeful present. He does this with reflections tinged both in the sadness and glory of his people at the way they kept their humanity in the terrible pain and suffering that they paid to survive the experience. He concludes with a ray of hope for a brighter American future. Where Larry Matsuda's poems weave this rich tapestry of personal experiences and emotions with his family and friends, they are manifestation of similar emotions, problems, and situations faced by most, if not all, of the nearly 120,000 persons of Japanese American ancestry who faced the Draconian measures that befell his family.

William Faulkner's words resonates here about the poet's and writer's duty that captures so well Larry Matsuda's ability to encapsulate the many difficult moments faced by the Issei and Nisei generations as they went through their daily struggles and moments of this period. Faulkner exhorts the writer, ". . . [to] teach himself that the basest of all things is to be afraid: and, teaching himself that, forget it forever, leaving no room in his workshop for anything but the old verities and truths of the heart, the universal truths lacking which any story is ephemeral and doomed—love and honor and pity and pride and compassion and sacrifice."[7]

Thus, although this dreadful American World War II saga is recorded in numerous historical accounts, social science analysis, art works, and novels, there exists fewer works of poetry. *A Cold Wind from Idaho* represents an important contribution to this Japanese American literature and specifically of the World War II American incarceration story. In the following poems, Larry Matsuda captures all these "truths" that William Faulkner entrusts to the newer generation of writers to contend with. Yet, to fully appreciate the nuanced aspects of many of the poems certain central motifs of the various poems must be understood.

The Matsuda family's World War II journey starts in Seattle, Washington. They along with 7,628 other Issei and Nisei were kept in the Western Washington Fairgrounds just outside of Puyallup, Washington, in an Assembly Center ironically known as "Camp Harmony." There, his Nisei father and mother carrying Larry, and his older Sansei brother comprised the Matsuda family. After their next move to the Minidoka, Idaho War Relocation Center, Larry was born. The poems reflect an adult perspective, but the focus shifts from childhood memories through the post-incarceration period to present-day reflections. Present-day social science research suggests the retention and behavioral display of various Japanese values passed through the generations – from Issei to the Sansei.[8] These Japanese values and norms, however, are not radically different from American middle class norms and many are compatible but not congruent with them: "politeness, the respect for authority and parental wishes, duty to the community, diligence, cleanliness and

---

7. Faulkner, William, Nobel Prize Speech, December 10, 1950, Stockholm, Sweden.17

8. Miyamoto, S. Frank, Stephen Fugita, and Tetsuden Kashima. "A Theory of Interpersonal Relations for Cross-Cultural Studies," Behaviormetrika, Vol. 29, 2002, 149-183 and Yamaoka, op.cit.

neatness, emphasis on personal achievement and on long-range goals, a sense of shame concerning non-sanctioned behavior, the importance of keeping up one's appearance, and a degree of 'outer-directness' are values shared by the two cultures."[9] Others values include a sense of personal reserve, reliance on inner strength, perseverance in the face of adversity, control over the display of inner emotions, respect for the family, careful attention to group and interpersonal harmonious relationships, and a marked degree of attention for the other's perception of oneself.[10]

These characteristics permeate the actions and relationship especially with Larry's Issei grandparents in "The Noble Thing," "First Memory", "Hummingbird" and the "Go Game." The Nisei values are expressed admirably in "They were Expendable" while the Sansei continuation of these values and norms are contained in numerous entries, especially with the metaphor of the Samurai, as a silent, honorable warrior, with the expressed desire to do what is right even at the cost of facing public censor. In "We are Defined by Rice," what a group values and treasures help to define what is important to the person. Some poems also ask for more information. In "1942 Nightmare," the neighbor Kazuko's sudden departure may be understood as a victim of the FBI arrests into the Department of Justice internment camps conducted in the weeks following the attack on Pearl Harbor.

As well, in "Hiroshima Family Graves, III" the Federal

---

9. Harry Kitano, *Japanese Americans: The Evolution of a Subculture*, Englewood Cliffs, NJ: Prentice-Hall, 2ND ED., 1976: 139; William Caudill, "Japanese American Personality and Acculturation," Genetic Psychological Monographs 45 (1952): 3-102; George DeVos, "A Quantitative Rorschach Assessment of Maladjustment and Rigidity in Acculturating Japanese Americans," Genetic Psychological Monographs 52 (1955): 51-58.18

10. Fugita, Stephan, S. Frank Miyamoto and Tetsuden Kashima, "Interpersonal Style and Japanese American Organizational Involvement," Behaviormetrika, Vol. 29, No. 2, 2002, 185-202.19

Bureau of Investigation arrived to arrest Larry's grandfather ["Ji-chan"] as a marked man perhaps similar to Kazuko's fate. The basis for his detention concerned his continued tie with Japan's wartime military – that his deceased son had been a high ranking naval officer. Refusing to allow the FBI agents to take her father, Larry's mother hustles him away from their apprehending arms. Nevertheless, the government prevailed as the reader sees later in "Go Game" as "Ji-chan" was in the WRA Minidoka, Idaho, center "after his release from a FBI [Department of Justice] camp."

In another poem, the universal concern of a mother's love for their children, especially in wartime, is poignantly expressed with an important Japanese cultural symbol in "Private First Class Harry." Cultures differ in where they symbolically express areas of vital reference. In America, for example, when we refer to ourselves, we usually point to our chest; in Japan, they usually point to their nose. Where Americans place especial symbolic importance to the heart, in Japan, the stomach is considered a vital yet vulnerable portion of one anatomy. Many Japanese in Japan don an extra layer of wrapping to ward off colds, illness, and other sicknesses and this poem introduces the "hara-maki," literally, a "stomach-wrapping," to which the mother in the poem carefully knits a wool wrap for her son to wear as a mother's armor of love. A more formal cultural armor sewn and sent to the Nisei soldiers by their mothers is the "sennin-bari" or literally, "thousand-people-needle." Here, a mother would take a white muslin stomach cloth and ask a thousand ladies each to sew a stitch creating a symbolic talisman for warriors going off to battle.[11] Stories are told even today where mothers in the WRA centers would traverse the camp requesting friends and passing

11. I am indebted to Mrs. Kuniko Takamura, for this information, Seattle, WA, December, 2009. In addition, since it is difficult to gather a thousand women to place a stitch each, a woman with the same birth year as the soldier may sew more than one stitch. Other informants states that a person born in the Tiger year of the Asian twelve-year cycle is also allowed more than one sew.

women to add a stitch to complete the "sennin-bari" which would then be sent to their young son for his personal safeguard while serving in the famed Japanese American segregated unit, the 442nd Regimental Combat Team or the less well known, but equally important, Military Intelligence Service.

Throughout the many poems there arises a clear perspective against the horrors of war. And the volume ends with "Arc De Triomphe, 2003 Invasion of Iraq," on the present mid-East conflict, but with a decided Japanese American perspective. Here, Larry Matsuda continues his perspective about the continual dilemma of an ethnic Japanese American – "wearing this yellow skin, I am unable to walk freely in my own country," all the while being an American Samurai outside its boundaries.

Through his poetry, Larry Matsuda opens the reader's eyes and heart to the personal consequences and realities of suffering wrought by the 1942 governmental gross misconduct on Japanese Americans. In 1981, the congressionally created Commission on Wartime Relocation and Internment of Civilians "review[ed] the facts and circumstances surrounding Executive Order Numbered 9066. . . and the impact of such Executive Order on American citizens and permanent resident aliens."[12] Their conclusion was brief: "In sum, Executive Order 9066 was not justified by military necessity, and the decisions that followed from it – exclusion, detention, the ending of detention and the ending of exclusion – were not founded upon military considerations. The broad historical causes that shaped these decisions were race prejudice, war hysteria and a failure of political leadership."[137] All persons of Japanese ancestry in the United States were vindicated by these findings and those

---

12. Report of the Commission on Wartime Relocation and Internment of Civilians, *Personal Justice Denied*, Seattle: University of Washington Press, 1997 (1982): 459.

13. Ibid.21

still living in 1988 that were directly affected by the authority of Executive Order 9066 received a Presidential apology and a monetary redress payment.

But an apology and money can only ease but never erase an ineradicable truth, that a group of Americans and their permanent resident parents were victims of a horrendous miscarriage of justice. The historical facts alone cannot express a mother's deep worry over her son's well-being knowing that her soldier son is equally worried about his parent's suffering while they are incarcerated in a primitive prison. Neither can it express the granddaughter's suffering when she hears of the terminal illness or death of a beloved grandparent with whom she cannot quickly visit since they reside in separate WRA centers. And none except the very young could escape the personal degradation and suffering that was so often etched on the faces of the adults as they met each day worried about the next heartless decision promulgated by their incarcerators. The poet's power rests in the ability to delve into the truth at the personal level that Larry Matsuda does so stunningly well.

Tetsuden [Tetsu] Kashima
University of Washington
Seattle, WA, 2010.
[Incarcerated, WRA "Relocation Center," 1942-1945]

Notes

1. In "Too Young to Remember", the Minidoka Relocation Center was one of ten World War II "relocation centers" internment or concentration camps during World War II for approximately 120,000 Japanese and Japanese Americans. The other camps were Poston Arizona, Tule Lake California, Manzanar California, Gila River Arizona, Rohwer Arkansas, Jerome Arkansas, Heart Mountain Wyoming, Topaz Utah, and Amache Colorado.

2. In "The Noble Thing", the line *that was a noble thing to do* is a direct quote attributed to Larry Matsuda in the July 9, 2006 Associated Press story "Return to Detention Camp Raises Old Hurts, New Plans" by Christopher Smith. The article was carried by 50 news services including one in the United Kingdom. The new plans refer to the restoration of the site, Minidoka WRA Camp, as a national historic site.

3. In "Burial at Washelli Cemetery", the New Year tai is a fish. It is either a Red Snapper or Sea Bream.

4. The quotation from Henry McLemore was from ten Broek, Jacobus, Edward N. Barnhart, and Floyd W. Matson. Prejudice, War, and the Constitution. Berkeley, California: University of California Press, 1968 (1954).

5. "Imagined President Roosevelt and the White House Cabinet Discussing the Sneak Attack on Pearl Harbor" refers to a government lottery after the war which awarded white veterans parcels of Minidoka farmland from the relocation camp, plus two and one half barracks. Returning Japanese American veterans were not eligible to participate.

6. In "Enola Gay and the Big Bomb", "Enola Gay" was the name of the B-29 airplane that dropped the atomic bomb on Hiroshima. The name of the bomb was Little Boy.

7. In "Hummingbird", "Ba-chan" is Japanese for grandmother.

8. In "They Were Expendable", a "Nisei" is a second generation Japanese American.

9. In "Bainbridge Island—They Were the First", "Ji-chan" is Japanese for grandfather. "Issei "is a first generation Japanese person and "Nisei" is a second generation Japanese American. Special thanks to Carole Koura Kubota and Dr. Frank Kitamoto for their stories of Bainbridge Island, Washington.

10. In "Go Game", "gohan" is cooked rice, "mochi" is pounded rice, and "gandy dancers" are railroad workers who pound spikes to lay rails. On the West Coast many of the gandy dancers were Japanese laborers. During the late 1800s Japanese worked on the railroads and mines in Wyoming, Oregon and Washington. For example, the Oregon Shortline Railroad employed 1,000 Japanese. In Sweetwater County Wyoming approximately 436 Japanese were employed, and at one time the Union Pacific made a concerted effort to replace Swedish laborers with Japanese because they were cheap labor. "Gaman" is a Japanese cultural value which encourages people to tolerate the intolerable with dignity. This concept made Japanese Americans silent partners to their own humiliation. It developed from Japan being a small crowded island with many deprivations at times, so that to complain would actually be seen as a prideful attack upon the community, keeping it from being able to bear the intolerable. It is also related to the samurai code of "Bushido" which encourages emotional detachment as a way to endure pain.

11. In "Roots—Lt. Ehren Watada", Lt. Watada refused deployment to Iraq. The 442nd Regimental Combat Team was composed of Japanese Americans who fought in Europe. They were a highly decorated unit of approximately 3,800 soldiers who rescued the Texas Lost Battalion surrounded in the Vosges mountains in Italy by Germans in 1944. After fighting for four days they rescued 211 Texans and suffered 800 causalities or about half its roster at that time. After the war, a Hollywood film starring Van Johnson entitled "Go for Broke" was released that chronicled their war experiences.

12. In "Blaine Methodist Church Presentation", a "katana" is a samurai sword. It is a long steel sword used for combat and represents the samurai's honor.

13. "FBI After 9-11" is based on a documentary video shown at the 2006 Minidoka Pilgrimage about the FBI invading a Muslim family's home. The film was shown to indicate that the racial and ethnic incursions of the American government against its citizens still continues.

14. "Daruma Maker" was written for my Uncle Tomokiyo Yamada who makes and collects darumas. A "daruma" is a Japanese doll that tips but never remains down and represents the qualities of optimism and determination. It has the power to grant wishes. When the wish is granted the eyes are colored in and the daruma should be destroyed because it served its purpose. Darumas originated several centuries ago in Takasaki City, Japan and were referenced in song as early as the 1600s.

15. "The Sun Ya Bar" refers to Roger Shimomura, an internationally-known artist who retired as a professor of art at Kansas University (KU), was a University Distinguished Professor and is currently a professor emeritus at KU. He graduated from

Seattle's Garfield High School and the University of Washington in Seattle. Although he lives in Kansas, he regularly spends time in New York and Seattle. Roger's art addresses racism in the USA and he has done several series on Minidoka and one inspired by his grandmother's diary during the relocation. She wrote extensively about her experiences at Camp Harmony Washington and the Minidoka Idaho Relocation Center. "Bushido" is the samurai or warrior's code of conduct that stresses honor and duty.

16. In Higo's Five and Dime, "sentos" are Japanese public bath houses and "Issei" are first generation Japanese. Issei were forbidden by law to become US citizens until 1952.

Sanzo and Matsuyo Murakami opened Higo's in 1932 and lived in the building. Chiyoko died in 1937. The Murakami family was interned in Mindioka, Idaho from 1942 to 1945 and the family reopened Higo's in 1945. Sanzo died in 1946, Matsuyo died in 1965, and Paul Murakami passed the legacy of Higo to John Bisbee and Binko Chiong Bisbee in 2004 to open Kobo's Gallery at Higo, which became a central community gathering place in Seattle's International District showing Japanese-American art, pottery, handcrafts and allowing writers and speakers for that community to present work there.

17. The source for "Reflections While Falling" was a newspaper article entitled "Slipping Fault May Increase Quake Risk" which appeared in the September 15th 2005 *Seattle Times*.

18. "Finding Morelia, Michoacán.de Ocampo" refers to Alfredo Arreguin, an internationally known artist who has lived and painted in Seattle for over 51 years. He was born in Morelia, Mexico. He has exhibited at the Smithsonian among many other prestigious galleries across America and is known for his complex pattern painting style. Our friendship began at a fund

raising breakfast for minority university students in Seattle. One evening at a dinner held at my home he told me and other guests of his joyous reunion with his father, after years of feeling discarded and unworthy. This became the occasion of my poem. Alfredo said his grandfather took him to las Canoas which is named after the Spanish for "canoes". I like the sound of Morelia better so I transported the trip to his birth place since being recognized by his father was a kind of new birth.

19. "Salmon Journey" refers to Tess Gallagher, an internationally known poet, editor and author. Her late husband, Raymond Carver, is a famous short story writer, essayist and poet. For over a year she kindly consented to mentor me in my work on this book.

20. In "Matsutake Tori", a "matsutake" is a "Ponderosa Pine mushroom" valued for its wonderful fragrance and firm texture.

21. In "Arc de Triomphe, 2003 Invasion of Iraq", "C'est la guerre" means "This is war". "Paris contre la guerre" means "Paris against the war". "Gaman" is a Japanese value which is to tolerate the intolerable with dignity, in other words: Silence. "En Amerique and En Paris" should be "A" with an accent mark and it should read "A Amerique" and "A Paris", but in the poem broken French is spoken.

Larry Matsuda was born in the Minidoka, Idaho War Relocation Center during World War II. He and his family along with 120,000 Japanese and Japanese Americans were held in ten concentration camps without a crime and without due process for approximately three years.

Matsuda has a Ph.D. in education and was recently a visiting professor at Seattle University. He was a junior high language arts teacher and Seattle School District administrator and principal for twenty-seven years.

He studied poetry under the late Professor Nelson Bentley at the University of Washington and has participated in the Castilla Poetry Reading Series there. He has read his poetry at numerous events in Washington, Oregon, and Idaho including the famous Kobo at Higo's venue in Seattle's International District with his mentor Tess Gallagher.

His poems appear in *Poets Against the War* website, *The Raven Chronicles, New Orleans Review, Floating Bridge Press, Cerise Press* and the *International Examiner Newspaper*. In 2005 he and two colleagues co-edited *Community and Difference: Teaching, Pluralism and Social Justice*, Peter Lang Publishing, New York. The book won the 2006 National Association of Multicultural Education Phillip Chinn Book Award.

He lives with his wife, Karen, and son, Matthew in Seattle, Washington and is a consultant presently helping to re-design schools as better physical learning environments.